Slow Cooker Meals Made Simple

Save Time, Eat Healthy, Feel Great

77 Slow Cooker Recipes

with Katie Bramlett

Slow Cooker Meals Made Simple

For information contact;
Warrior Media Inc.
c/o The Warrior Wife
PO Box 1499, Soquel CA 95073
www.thewarriorwife.com

Cover Photo by Julie Cahill Photography
Book and Cover design by Andrea Horowitt & Ben Chargin
Editing by Beth Chargin, CD Johnson, Marina Martinez
Content Contributor Kaitie Korver

Property of Warrior Media, Inc.
ISBN: 9780997770308
First Edition: July 2016
10 9 8 7 6 5 4 3 2 1

About Me

What you need to know about me is that I used to be a horrible cook. I could never get a recipe to turn out right, and I actually relied on my husband to do most of the cooking. I was tired of feeling insecure about my skillset in the kitchen and decided to find a solution.

Here's what I was doing wrong: I was under the impression that if I wanted to cook healthy, I basically had to be a chef. NOT TRUE! It turns out, I was overcomplicating the whole idea. Once I could bring it back to the basics, things really turned around for me in the kitchen.

The slow cooker has been an AMAZING tool for me! In fact, cooking healthy has never been easier. If I'm having a busy week, I can simply collect the ingredients and throw them in the slow cooker. By the end of the day, it's ready and I have no excuses for not eating a healthy, home-cooked meal.

A super helpful tip: Double the recipe and store the extra in the freezer. You'll have a healthy meal ready to go!

My Take on "Eating Healthy"

Things in our culture have become so confusing around "what is healthy?" and I want to make it as simple as possible for you. My personal philosophy is not centered around complicated research (although there is research to support my theory), it's based on the idea that human beings were designed to eat pretty simply. The processed food movement has made simple eating extremely confusing for most of us. Bottom line, if it comes ready-to-eat in a box or a package, it's probably not that great for you.

Humans have been hunters and gathers for centuries, eating basic foods such as meats, fruits, vegetables, tubers, herbs, and so on. We've moved away from this "real food" model into a complex, processed food, fad-dieting society. If you're trying to figure out what is healthy, just make it easy on yourself and ask, "is this a real food?" Once you get past that, you can go on to more complex questions about things like organic foods, meat quality, and best dairy options. I go over these below.

With all of that said, I want to share with you one of my favorite Chinese proverbs:

"It's better to eat bad food and feel good than to eat good food and feel bad."

I'm a big believer in balance. There've been times in my life where I let my need for perfect nutrition cause a lot of unnecessary stress. I find that I'm a lot happier if I allow myself to bend the rules once in awhile. This doesn't mean you fly off the handle and eat a box of doughnuts because it's the weekend and you ate healthy all week. This means that you seek balance and allow yourself some freedom with foods that work for you. There's a way to be smart about it. For example, a scoop of organic ice cream on a Saturday night is way better than a whole box of cookies. The bottom line is that it needs to make sense for YOU. If you're struggling with a major health challenge, you may be in a space where bending the rules every once in awhile isn't possible until you are in a better space. Listen to your body; it knows the way.

Why Organic?

I'm a firm believer in looking at nutrition in the most simple way possible. I ask myself, "how is food supposed to be?" and "how was my body designed to process food for optimal health?" When I ask myself these questions, it's pretty easy to find the answers. If I have the choice between a fruit covered in pesticides and one that was simply grown in it's natural state, I'm going with the organic option.

Why I Include Dairy

I've been super lucky in the sense that my body does great with most dairy. I know this is not the case for other people. If your body doesn't feel well after eating dairy, you should probably avoid it. The good news is there is a lot of great alternatives today, such as almond milk or coconut milk. I do personally avoid soy milk because of its estrogen-promoting nature.

Why I Buy Full-Fat Dairy Products

When I do eat dairy, I choose to buy full-fat dairy products. This goes back to my question about nutrition in general: How is food supposed to be? Did the milk come out of the cow fat-free? Buying full-fat dairy products means you're buying food that is less processed. Also—and I know it's hard to believe—but fat is actually good for you. The only thing you need to remember about this is, not all fats are created equal. I'll make it easy and provide you with a list of healthy fats and others to avoid.

Why Quality Dairy Products Are a Big Deal

It pays to buy quality dairy products. This is a big deal if you're going to be including dairy in your diet. Unfortunately, most dairy products contain unnecessary hormones and other preservatives that can be harmful to your family. The best type of dairy you can buy is full-fat, organic, and grass-fed. This simply means that the animals' nutrition came from roaming around on a farm eating grass, rather than grains and other processed foods.

Healthy Fats

- Animal fats (from good, organic sources)
- Olive oil (from good, organic sources)
- Coconut oil (from good, organic sources)
- Avocado oil (from good, organic sources)
- Butter (from organic, grass-fed cows)
- Ghee (from organic, grass-fed cows)
  *smoke points vary

Fats to Avoid

- Any type of seed oil (like sunflower or sesame)
- Hydrogenated oils (like shortening or margarine)
- Any type of "cooking oils" (other than what is listed above)

Selecting Meats

I wish going to the store and buying a pound of high-quality, healthy beef was a no-brainer. Unfortunately, our food system has become a big business, and mass production has become the priority. With mass production meat products, most animals are kept in small, confined spaces and they eat a highly processed, grain-based diet. This is not how these animals evolved to live, and it doesn't produce a high-quality, nutrient-dense product for the consumer. If you're avoiding processed grains, but eat an animal that lived on such food, there's no avoiding it: you're eating that too.

The Best Type of Meat to Purchase

- 100% grass-fed or pastured-raised beef or lamb
- Organic, free-range chicken
- Organic, nitrate-free pork
- Wild-caught seafood (farm-raised seafood falls along the same lines as a "processed food")

Canned Foods

Researchers are discovering a whole laundry list of negative side effects linked to BPA, which can be found in plastics and canned goods. Rather than going into that here, I'm just going to tell you that you're better off avoiding them. Some of the recipes in this book call for canned ingredients, and I want to mention that when possible, search for cans labeled "BPA Free."

Table of Contents

Breakfast

Beef

Chicken

Chicken (cont'd)

Lamb

Pork

Seafood

Vegetables

Dessert

BREAKFAST

Slow Cooker Cherry Almond Oats

Prep time: 10 minutes | Cook time: about 6 hours | Serves 4

Ingredients:

- 1 apple
- 2 cups full-fat coconut milk
- 1 cup uncooked gluten-free steel cut oats
- ¾ cup dried tart cherries, no sugar added
- 1 ½ Tbsp. unsalted butter
- 1 ½ cups water
- ½ tsp. almond extract
- ¼ tsp. salt

Optional for serving: toasted sliced almonds, additional coconut milk, or grass-fed butter.

Directions:

1. Add all ingredients (except optional toppings) to the slow cooker.
2. Stir and cook on Low for about 6 hours. Serve with any desired toppings.

Slow Cooker Granola

Prep time: 10 minutes | Cook time: 3-4 hours | Serves 4

Ingredients:

- 4 Tbsp. salted butter or coconut oil, melted
- 5 cups uncooked gluten-free rolled oats
- ½ cup honey
- ½ cup dried fruit, no sugar added
- 2 Tbsp. flax seeds
- ¼ cup slivered almonds
- ¼ cup pumpkin seeds
- ¼ cup raw sunflower seeds
- ¼ cup raw unsweetened organic coconut

Directions:

1. Place all the dry ingredients into the slow cooker.
2. Melt the butter or coconut oil and add to dry ingredients.
3. Stir in the honey; mix well.
4. Cook on High for 3 to 4 hours and stir often. Keep the lid ajar so some of the moisture can easily escape.

Slow Cooker Apple Coffee Cake

Prep time: 20 minutes | Cook time: 2-3.5 hours | Serves 6

Ingredients:

- 2 apples, diced
- 2 cups gluten-free baking mix
- 1 egg
- 2 Tbsp. butter, melted
- 2/3 cup applesauce, no sugar added
- ¼ cup full-fat coconut milk
- 1 tsp. cinnamon
- 1 tsp. vanilla extract

Streusel topping:

- ¼ cup gluten-free baking mix
- ¼ cup coconut sugar
- 2 Tbsp. grass-fed butter, softened
- ¼ cup nuts of your choice, finely chopped

Directions:

1. Lightly grease the inside of the slow cooker with coconut oil.

2. In a mixing bowl, combine all the ingredients for the coffee cake. Pour mix into slow cooker and smooth out the top.

3. In a small bowl, combine the remaining ingredients for the streusel topping and sprinkle evenly on top of the batter.

4. Cook on High for 2 to 3 hours or until the cake is golden brown and pulls away from the sides of the slow cooker. Remove the lid and cook on High for another 30 minutes, or until a toothpick comes out clean when inserted in the center.

Slow Cooker Eggs and Potatoes

Prep time: 15 minutes | Cook time: 6-8 hours | Serves 4

Ingredients:

- ½ lb. sausage, cooked and diced
- 6 baby potatoes, diced
- 2 cups vegetables, diced
- 2 cloves garlic, minced
- 8 eggs
- 1 ½ cups shredded cheese
- 1 cup milk
- Salt and freshly ground pepper, to taste

Directions:

1. Whisk everything together.
2. Cook on Low for 6 to 8 hours, or until the center is puffed and firm when gently pressed.

Slow Cooker Breakfast Casserole

Prep time: 20 minutes | Cook time: 6-8 hours | Serves 4

Ingredients:

- 1 lb. uncured bacon, pre-cooked and crumbled
- 2 lbs. potatoes, grated (frozen hash browns can work too)
- 2 cloves garlic, minced
- 1 red bell pepper, diced
- 1 onion diced
- 12 eggs
- 8 oz. shredded cheese
- 1 cup milk
- salt and freshly ground pepper, to taste

Directions:

1. Add half of the potatoes or hash browns to the bottom of the slow cooker.
2. Add half of everything else, then repeat.
3. In a bowl, whisk the eggs and milk together with salt and pepper.
4. Pour over the casserole and cook on Low for 6 to 8 hours, until the center is puffed and is firm when pressed.

Slow Cooker Breakfast Quinoa

Prep time: 20 minutes | Cook time: 2 hours | Serves 4

Ingredients:

- 6 Medjool dates, chopped
- 1 apple, diced
- 1 cup quinoa
- ¼ cup pecans, chopped
- 3 cups milk (coconut or almond milk work well too)
- 2 tsp. cinnamon
- 1 tsp. vanilla extract
- ¼ tsp. salt
- ¼ tsp. nutmeg

Optional for serving: fresh fruit, additional milk, or nuts.

Directions:

1. Put all the ingredients in the slow cooker.
2. Cook on High for 2 hours or until all the liquid is absorbed. Serve with any optional toppings if desired.

Slow Cooker Greek Frittata

Ingredients:

- ¼ cup green onions, sliced
- 8 eggs, whisked
- 6 oz. feta cheese, crumbled
- 1 (14 oz.) can artichoke hearts, drained and cut into small pieces
- 1 (12 oz.) jar roasted red peppers, drained and cut into small pieces
- ¼ cup olives, sliced
- Salt and freshly ground pepper, to taste

Directions:

1. Lightly oil the inside of the slow cooker. Whisk all ingredients together until well combined, then pour into the slow cooker.
2. Cook on Low for 2 to 3 hours or until the eggs are puffed and the center is firm to the touch.

Slow Cooker Quinoa Bars

Prep time: 10 minutes | Cook time: 3-4 hours | Serves 8

Ingredients:

- ½ cup Medjool dates, chopped
- 2 eggs
- 2 Tbsp. chia seeds
- 2 Tbsp. creamy almond butter
- 2 Tbsp. maple syrup
- 1 cup full-fat coconut milk
- 1/3 cup almonds, roasted and chopped
- 1/3 cup dried apricots (no sugar added)
- ½ tsp. cinnamon
- Pinch of salt
- 1/3 cup quinoa

Directions:

1. Lightly oil the slow cooker with coconut oil and cut a piece of parchment to fit on the bottom.

2. In a bowl, combine the almond butter and maple syrup, melt until the almond butter is creamy. Then whisk the coconut milk, cinnamon, and salt. Mix until all ingredients are well incorporated.

3. Whisk in the eggs until well combined, and then mix in all the remaining ingredients.

4. Pour the batter into the slow cooker and cook on LOW until the top of the bars just appear to set, about 3 to 4 hours.

5. Run a knife around the edge of the bars and remove from the slow cooker.

6. Place in the refrigerator to cool completely before cutting. Store in the refrigerator.

Slow Cooker Huevos Rancheros

Prep time: 5-10 minutes | Cook time: about 2.5 hours | Serves 6-8

Ingredients:
- 10oz. salsa
- 1 clove garlic, mined
- 12oz. Monterey jack cheese, shredded
- 10 eggs
- 1 cup milk (coconut or almond milk work well too)
- 8 gluten-free tortillas
- Coconut oil, for greasing
- 1 (4oz.) can diced green chilies, drained
- ½ tsp. ancho chili powder
- Salt and fresh ground pepper

Optional for serving: green onions, sour cream, thinly sliced cabbage, avocado, cilantro, lime, or additional salsa.

Directions:
1. In a large bowl, whisk the eggs with the milk, 8 ounces of the cheese, salt and pepper, chili powder, garlic, and chilies.
2. Pour into the slow cooker and cook on Low for 2 hours. Check once in a while to make sure the edges aren't burning.
3. Pour the taco sauce or salsa over the eggs. Spread it out evenly across the top, then sprinkle the remaining 4 ounces of cheese over the top and cook for another 15 to 20 minutes.

Serve over warmed gluten-free tortillas and top with additional toppings, if desired.

BEEF

Slow Cooker Sloppy Joes

Prep time: 20 minutes | Cook time: 4-6 hours | Serves 4

Ingredients:
- 2 lbs. ground beef or turkey
- 4 cloves of garlic, minced
- 1 ½ cups cremini mushrooms, minced
- 1 onion, mined
- 1 red bell pepper, finely chopped
- 2 cans tomato sauce, no sugar added
- 2 Tbsp. honey
- 2 Tbsp. gluten-free Worcestershire sauce
- 1 Tbsp. mustard
- 1 Tbsp. apple cider vinegar
- 1 Tbsp. chili powder
- Salt and freshly ground pepper

Optional for serving: Butter lettuce leaves in place of a bun.

Directions:
1. In a large skillet over medium-high heat, brown the ground beef with the onion garlic. Break it up into small pieces as it cooks and drain off the fat.
2. Add the beef to the slow cooker and add the remaining ingredients. Cook on Low for 4 to 6 hours.
3. Serve with buns or butter lettuce in place of buns.

Slow Cooker Basic Pot Roast

Prep time: 20 minutes | Cook time: 6-8 hours | Serves 8

Ingredients:

- 3 to 4lbs. beef chuck roast
- 8 cloves garlic, minced
- 2 onions, roughly chopped
- 1 ½ cups baby carrots
- 1 cup parsnips, peeled and cut into 1" pieces
- 3 cups beef stock
- 1 Tbsp. coconut oil
- 1 (8 oz.) can tomato sauce
- 2 bay leaves
- 1 ½ tsp. chili powder
- 1 ½ tsp. dried thyme
- ½ tsp. salt
- ¼ tsp. pepper

Directions:

1. Sprinkle roast with salt and pepper.
2. Over medium-high heat, sear the roast in coconut oil on all sides.
3. Transfer to a 6-qt. slow cooker. Add in the garlic, carrots, parsnips, stock, tomato sauce, bay leaves, thyme and chili powder.
4. Cover and cook on Low for 6 to 8 hours or until the meat is tender.

Slow Cooker Pomegranate Short Ribs

Prep time: 20 minutes | Cook time: about 8 hours | Serves 3-4

Ingredients:

- 4lbs. beef short ribs
- 4 cloves garlic, minced
- 1 onion, thinly sliced
- 4 cups beef stock
- 4 Tbsp. coconut oil
- 4 Tbsp. maple syrup
- 1 cup pomegranate juice, no sugar added
- ¼ cup coconut aminos
- Garlic powder, to taste
- Salt and freshly ground pepper, to taste

Directions:

1. Preheat oven to 325°F. Melt 2 Tbsp. of coconut oil in a large skillet over medium-high heat. Season short ribs on all sides with salt, pepper, and garlic powder. Brown on all sides, and then place in the slow cooker. You'll have to do this in batches.

2. Add onion and garlic to the pan and cook for about 3 minutes. Add the stock, pomegranate juice, coconut aminos, and maple syrup to the pan and bring it to a boil.

3. Once boiling, pour over the ribs into the slow cooker and cook on Low for 8 hours.

Place all glaze ingredients in a small pot and bring to a boil. Lower the heat to a simmer and allow it to reduce and thicken until it coats the back of a spoon. Carefully remove short ribs from the slow cooker and top with the glaze.

Slow Cooker Thai Beef Curry

Prep time: 20 minutes | Cook time: 6-8 hours | Serves 8

Ingredients:

- 3 lbs. stew meat
- 3 carrots, peeled and cut in 2-inch pieces
- 2 sweet potatoes, peeled and cut in large cubes
- 2 cloves garlic, minced
- 1 onion, chopped
- 1 lime, juiced
- 1 Tbsp. fresh ginger, grated
- 3 Tbsp. coconut oil
- 2 Tbsp. Thai curry paste (any color)
- 1 can full-fat coconut milk
- 1 Tbsp. honey
- 1 Tbsp. fish sauce
- 2 Tbsp. coconut aminos
- 2 tsp. salt

Directions:

1. In a large skillet, melt 1 tablespoon of coconut oil over medium-high heat and seat the beef. Season it with salt and place in the slow cooker. You'll have to do this in a few batches. Add the vegetables to the slow cooker as well.

2. Once the meat is done, melt another tablespoon of coconut oil on the same pan, add the garlic and curry paste. Stir around until fragrant, and then add the coconut milk, coconut aminos, lime juice, honey, and fish sauces. Whisk together, pour over the beef and vegetables, and set on Low to cook for 6 to 8 hours.

Serve over rice or cauliflower rice, and top with cilantro, green onions, cabbage, fresh lime juice and so on.

Slow Cooker Lasagna

Prep time: 20 minutes | Cook time: 4-6 hours | Serves 4-6

Ingredients:

- 1 ½ lb. ground beef
- 6 zucchinis, sliced very thin lengthwise, like lasagna noodles
- 2 large vine tomatoes, chopped
- 2 Tbsp. fresh basil, thinly sliced
- 1 Tbsp. cloves garlic, minced
- ½ onion, minced
- 2 eggs
- 1 ½ cup ricotta or cottage cheese
- 1 ½ cup mozzarella cheese
- 3 cups tomato sauce, no sugar added
- 1 ½ Tbsp. rosemary
- 1 ½ Tbsp. Italian seasoning

Directions:

1. Slice the zucchini, either by hand or with a mandolin. Put the slices on a paper towel to soak up the extra moisture.

2. In a large skillet over medium heat, add the beef. Break into pieces and stir frequently. Add the onion, garlic, and seasonings. Cook until the meat is fully cooked, and then add the tomatoes and sauce. Stir thoroughly and season to taste with salt and pepper. Simmer for about 5 minutes.

3. Mix the eggs and ricotta/cottage cheese in a bowl and set aside. In the slow cooker, add a little meat sauce and then some zucchini strips, and then the cottage cheese mixture. Repeat. Add the meat sauce to the top layer of zucchini and then cover with mozzarella. Cook on Low for 4 to 6 hours.

Slow Cooker Osso Bucco

Prep time: 20 minutes | Cook time: 6-8 hours | Serves 4

Ingredients:

- 3lbs. beef shanks, cut into 2-inch slices
- 3 cloves garlic, minced
- 1 cup carrot, diced
- 1 cup celery, diced
- 1 onion, diced
- 1 Tbsp. fresh thyme, minced
- 4 Tbsp. unsalted butter or coconut oil
- 2 Tbsp. tomato paste
- 1 (14 oz.) can diced tomatoes
- 1 cup dry white wine
- 1 cup beef stock
- 2 bay leaves
- Salt and freshly ground pepper, to taste

Directions:

1. Pat meat dry and season with salt and pepper. Melt a tablespoon of butter in a large skillet over medium heat and brown the shank slices on both sides. Remove and place in the slow cooker.

2. Add everything else to the slow cooker and cook on Low for 6 to 8 hours. Once the meat is done cooking, take the liquid out of the slow cooker and place in a pot on the stove. Bring to a boil and allow to reduce by half.

Once the sauce is reduced and thickened, pour over the meat and serve.

Slow Cooker Tomato Balsamic Pot Roast

Prep time: 10 minutes | Cook time: 8 hours | Serves 4-6

Ingredients:

- 1 chuck roast
- 4 cloves garlic, mined
- 1 onion, diced
- 1 (14 oz.) can fire-roasted tomatoes
- ¾ cup balsamic vinegar
- 1 tsp. salt
- 1 tsp. freshly ground pepper
- 1 tsp. chili powder
- 1 tsp. onion powder
- 1 tsp. garlic powder
- 1 tsp. paprika

Optional for serving: Additional vegetables or salad and mashed potatoes.

Directions:

1. Place onion and garlic in the bottom of the slow cooker.
2. Mix all the spices in a bowl and rub on the roast on all sides. Put the roast on top of the vegetables. Add the tomatoes and vinegar to the slow cooker and cook on Low for 8 hours.
3. Serve with roasted vegetables or salad and mashed potatoes, if desired.

Slow Cooker Beef Shanks

Prep time: 15 minutes | Cook time: 8 hours | Serves 4-6

Ingredients:

- 2 to 3 center-cut beef shanks
- 6 cloves garlic, roughly chopped
- 2 lbs. cabbage, roughly chopped
- 2 onions, chopped
- ½ lb. carrots, cut into 2-inch pieces
- ½ lb. cremini mushrooms, cut in half
- 1 (15 oz.) can diced tomatoes
- 1 cup chicken stock
- 3 bay leaves
- Salt and freshly ground pepper, to taste

Directions:

1. Place the onion, garlic, bay leaves, mushrooms, and cabbage in the slow cooker. Liberally season the beef shanks with salt and pepper, and then place on top of the veggies.
2. Set slow cooker on Low and cook for about 8 hours, or until the meat is tender.
3. Remove the meat and bones from the slow cooker, and season the stew with salt and pepper if necessary. Add the meat back to the pot and serve.

Slow Cooker Mexican Beef Stew

Prep time: 10 minutes | Cook time: 6-8 hours | Serves 4-6

Ingredients:

- 2 to 3 lbs. stew meat or chuck roast, cut into 2-inch pieces
- 3 cloves garlic
- 1 onion, roughly chopped
- 1 cup salsa verde
- 2 Tbsp. cumin
- 2 Tbsp. dried oregano
- 2 tsp. salt
- 1 ½ Tbsp. chili powder
- 1 Tbsp. smoked paprika

Directions:

1. Place the beef in the slow cooker, sprinkle on all the dry spices, and stir to coat. Add the salsa verde and mix well.
2. Cook on Low for 6 to 8 hours on High for 4 to 6 hours.
3. Use two forks to shred the meat once it's cooked and serve in bowls with your toppings of choice.

Slow Cooker Beef Tagine

Prep time: 20 minutes | Cook time: 6-8 hours | Serves 4

Ingredients:
- 2 lbs. chuck roast or stew meat, cut into 1-inch cubes
- 3 cloves garlic, minced
- 1 small to medium butternut squash, peeled and cut into ½-inch cubes
- 1 onion, diced
- ¼ cup fresh cilantro, optional for serving
- 2 Tbsp. coconut oil
- 1 cup tomato sauce, no sugar added
- ½ cup beef or chicken stock
- 1 tsp. cinnamon
- 1 tsp. garlic powder
- ½ tsp. chili powder
- ¼ tsp. cayenne
- Salt and freshly ground pepper, to taste

Optional for serving: Basmati rice or cauliflower rice.

Directions:
1. Season the meat with salt, pepper, cinnamon, garlic powder, chili powder, and cayenne.
2. Melt 2 tablespoons of coconut oil in a large skillet over medium-high heat and seat the beef on all sides. Add the slow cooker with the rest of the ingredients and cook on Low for 6 to 8 hours.

Serve with rice or cauliflower rice and fresh cilantro on top, if desired.

Slow Cooker Beef Bourguignon

Prep time: 20 minutes | Cook time: 6-8 hours | Serves 4-6

Ingredients:
- 1 ½ lbs. grass-fed stew meat, cubed
- 4 cloves garlic, minced
- 3 carrots, chopped
- 2 stalks celery, chopped
- 2 sprigs fresh thyme
- 1 onion, diced
- 1 sprig fresh rosemary
- 3 Tbsp. coconut oil
- 2 Tbsp. tomato paste
- 1 cup red wine
- 1 tsp. arrowroot powder
- ½ cup chicken stock
- 2 bay leaves
- Salt and freshly ground pepper, to taste

Directions:
1. In a large skillet, melt coconut oil. Brown meat on all sides. (You'll have to do this in a few batches.)
2. Add all the remaining ingredients to the slow cooker and place the meat on top. Whisk together the stock and arrowroot powder. Add this mixture to the pot and mix everything.
3. Set on Low for 6 to 8 hours.

Slow Cooker Corned Beef

Prep time: 10 minutes | Cook time: 7-8 hours | Serves 4-6

Ingredients:

- 4 lbs. corned beef brisket or round
- 2 lbs. fingerling potatoes
- 1 lb. carrots, peeled and cut into 3-inch pieces
- ½ head green cabbage, cores and roughly chopped
- ¼ lbs. pearl onions, peeled
- 1 Tbsp. apple cider vinegar
- 2 bay leaves
- Salt and freshly ground pepper, to taste

Optional for serving: Whole grain mustard.

Directions:

1. Place the ingredients in the slow cooker, starting with the potatoes on the bottom and finishing with the beef on the top.

2. Add enough water to the slow cooker to come halfway up the beef. Cook on Low for 7 to 8 hours. Take the meat out of the slow cooker and allow it to rest about 10 minutes before slicing. Serve with the other vegetables in the slow cooker and some whole grain mustard, if desired.

Slow Cooker Cabbage Soup

Prep time: 20 minutes | Cook time: 6-7 hours | Serves 4

Ingredients:
- 2 lbs. ground beef or turkey
- 3 cloves garlic, minced
- 2 shallots, minced
- 1 large head green cabbage
- ½ head cauliflower, processed into rice-sized pieces
- 16 oz. marinara sauce, no sugar added
- 4 to 6 cups beef or chicken stock
- 2 Tbsp. coconut oil
- ½ onion, diced
- 1 tsp. dried parsley
- 2 bay leaves
- 1 tsp. salt
- 1 tsp. freshly ground pepper
- ½ tsp. oregano

Directions:
1. Melt the coconut oil in a large skillet over medium heat and sauté the garlic, onion, and shallots. Add the beef and break it up into small pieces. Once it's almost cooked through, add it to the slow cooker.

Stir in the seasoning, marinara, cauliflower, cabbage, and stock. Mix well and cook on High for 2 to 3 hours or on Low for 6 to 7 hours.

Slow Cooker Taco Soup

Prep time: 20 minutes | Cook time: 4-6 hours | Serves 4

Ingredients:

- 1 lb. ground beef or turkey
- 2 cloves garlic, minced
- 2 bell pepper, diced
- 1 onion, diced
- 1 cup zucchini, diced
- ½ or 1 jalapeños, seeded and minced
- 4 cups chicken stock
- 2 (4.5 oz.) cans green chilies
- 1 (28 oz.) can diced tomatoes
- 1 can chipotle peppers in adobo sauce, chopped
- 1 tsp. chili powder
- 1 tsp. cumin
- ½ tsp. coriander
- Salt and freshly ground pepper, to taste

Optional for serving: Jalapeño slices, cilantro, avocado, cheese, cabbage or avocado.

Directions:

1. In a large skillet, brown the ground meat and break it up into large pieces. Drain the fat and add the meat to the slow cooker.

2. Add the remaining ingredients and cook on Low for 4 to 6 hours. Serve with the toppings of your choice.

Slow Cooker Short Ribs

Prep time: 20 minutes | Cook time: 6-8 hours | Serves 4

Ingredients:

- 4 lbs. beef short ribs, cut in half
- 4 carrots, chopped
- 2 stalks celery, chopped
- 2 cloves garlic, minced
- 1 onion, chopped
- 2 ½ cups beef stock
- 2 Tbsp. tomato paste
- 1 cup dry red wine
- 1 tsp. allspice
- Salt and freshly ground pepper, to taste

Directions:

1. In a large zip top bag, combine ½ cup of the beef stock with the garlic, allspice, salt and pepper, and then add the ribs and marinate in the refrigerator for 6 to 8 hours.
2. In the slow cooker, add the carrots, onion, celery, tomato paste, wine and stock. Add the meat and marinade. Cook on Low for 6 to 8 hours until the meat falls off the bone.

Slow Cooker Pineapple Chili

Prep time: 20 minutes | Cook time: 4-6 hours | Serves 6-8

Ingredients:

- 2 lbs. ground beef
- 1 lb. bacon, diced
- 4 cloves garlic, minced
- 2 onions, diced
- 2 bell peppers (any color), diced
- 1 jalapeño, diced (remove the seeds if you want it less spicy)
- 1 (20 oz.) can diced pineapple

- 1 (15 oz.) can tomato sauce
- 1 (15 oz.) can fire-roasted tomatoes
- 2 tsp. cumin
- ¼ cup chili powder
- Salt and freshly ground pepper, to taste

Directions:

1. Cook the bacon in a large skillet over medium heat. Remove from the pan once crispy, but leave the fat behind and partially cook the ground beef.

Drain the fat and add the bacon to the slow cooker, as well as the rest of the ingredients. Stir well and cook on Low for 4 to 6 hours.

Slow Cooker Barbacoa

Prep time: 10 minutes | Cook time: 8-9 hours | Serves 4-6

Ingredients:

- 1 ½ to 2 lbs. chuck roast
- 8 cloves garlic, mined
- 3 bay leaves
- 1 onion, chopped
- 2 chipotle peppers in adobo sauce, chopped
- 1 Tbsp. adobo sauce (from the can of chipotle peppers)
- ¼ cup apple cider vinegar
- ¼ cup chicken stock
- 1 Tbsp. cumin
- Salt and freshly ground pepper, to taste

For after cooking:

- 1 (16 oz.) can tomato sauce
- 1 (12 oz.) can green chilies
- 1 tsp. chipotle chili powder
- 1 tsp. cayenne
- 1tsp. red pepper
- ½ tsp. smoked paprika
- ½ tsp. nutmeg
- ¼ tsp. cloves
- Salt and freshly ground pepper, to taste

Directions:

1. Add the first of ingredients to the slow cooker and toss to coat. Cook on Low for 8 hours.
2. Once the roast is done cooking, use forks to shred the meat in the slow cooker. Throw away the bay leaves and add in the second set of ingredients. Mix well and cook on High for an additional 30 to 60 minutes.

Slow Cooker BBQ Brisket

Prep time: 10 minutes | Cook time: 7-8 hours | Serves 4-6

Ingredients:

- 3 lbs. brisket
- 10 to 12 oz. tomato paste
- 4 Tbsp. maple syrup
- 3 Tbsp. apple cider vinegar
- 2 Tbsp. coconut aminos
- 1 cup chicken stock
- 2 Tbsp. chili powder
- 1 Tbsp. garlic powder
- 1 Tbsp. salt

Directions:

1. Place all the ingredients except the brisket into the slow cooker and stir well. Add the meat and toss to coat.

Cook on Low for 7 to 8 hours. Serve with a salad, vegetables, or roasted sweet potatoes, if desired.

Slow Cooker Beanless Chili

Prep time: 20 minutes | Cook time: 4-6 hours | Serves 6-8

Ingredients:

- 1 ½ to 2 lbs. ground beef
- ½ lbs. uncured bacon
- 4 cloves garlic, minced
- 1 sweet onion, diced
- 1 lb. sweet potatoes, cubed
- 1 lb. butternut squash, diced
- 1 (14 oz.) can fire-roasted diced tomatoes
- 1 (4 oz.) can tomato paste
- 1 Tbsp. smoked paprika
- 1 Tbsp. chili powder
- 1 tsp. salt
- ½ tsp. freshly ground pepper
- ½ tsp. chipotle powder

Directions:

1. In a large skillet over medium heat, cook the bacon until crispy. Set the bacon aside and cook the beef. Break it up into pieces then add it to the slow cooker in addition to the other ingredients.
2. Set on Low and cook for 4 to 6 hours. Serve with the crispy bacon on top.

Slow Cooker Two Bean Chili

Prep time: 20 minutes | Cook time: 5-6 hours | Serves 4-6

Ingredients:
- 2 lbs. ground beef
- 4 cloves garlic, minced
- 1 onion, chopped
- 1 carrot, chopped
- 1 stalk celery, chopped
- 2 ¼ cup chicken stock
- 2 Tbsp. gluten-free Worcestershire sauce
- 1 (14 oz.) can fire-roasted tomatoes
- 1 (14 oz.) can Borlotti beans
- 2 (14 oz.) can cannellini beans
- 2 Tbsp. chili powder
- Red pepper flakes, to taste
- Salt and freshly ground pepper, to taste

Directions:
1. In a large pan, cook the beef, stirring often to break into pieces. Once it's about halfway cooked, add the onion and garlic. Cook until the onion is translucent.
2. Drain the beef and then add the mixture to the slow cooker. Add the Worcestershire sauce, tomatoes, red pepper flakes, chili powder, salt, chopped carrot, celery, and stock. Cook on Low for 5 to 6 hours, and in the last 30 minutes, add the beans.

Slow Cooker Pot Roast with Mushroom Gravy

Prep time: 20 minutes | Cook time: 6-8 hours | Serves 4-6

Ingredients:

- 2 lbs. chuck roast
- 8 oz. cremini mushrooms, sliced
- 6 cloves garlic, minced
- 2 onions, roughly chopped
- 3 to 4 cups beef stock
- ½ cup full-fat coconut milk
- 1 tsp. garlic powder
- 1 tsp. onion powder
- ½ tsp. paprika
- Salt and freshly ground pepper, to taste

Directions:

1. In the slow cooker, combine the beef stock, coconut milk, onions, garlic, mushrooms, and spices. Make a well in the center to place the roast.
2. Cook on Low for 6 to 8 hours.

CHICKEN

Slow Cooker Teriyaki Chicken

Prep time: 10 minutes | Cook time: 4-5 hours | Serves 4

Ingredients:

- 2 lbs. chicken thighs, skinless and boneless
- 2 cloves garlic, minced
- 1 Tbsp. fresh ginger, grated
- 1 Tbsp. honey
- ½ cup pineapple juice, no sugar added
- ½ cup coconut aminos
- 2 tsp. onion powder
- Salt and freshly ground pepper, to taste

Directions:

1. Sprinkle the chicken with salt and pepper and put in the slow cooker. Combine the remaining ingredients in a bowl and pour over the chicken.
2. Cook on Low for 4 to 5 hours and serve.

Slow Cooker Taco Chicken

Prep time: 10 minutes | Cook time: 6-8 hours | Serves 4

Ingredients:
- 1 ½ lbs. chicken breast
- 2 tsp. chili powder
- 1 ½ cups chicken stock
- 1 ½ tsp. smoked paprika
- 1 ½ tsp. cumin
- 1 tsp. onion powder
- 1 tsp. garlic powder
- Salt and freshly ground pepper

Optional for serving: Lime juice, cilantro, shredded cabbage or lettuce, avocado, beans, sour cream, shredded cheese.

Directions
1. Place the chicken in the slow cooker and cover the chicken with spices.
2. Cook for 3 to 4 hours on High, or about 6 to 8 hours on Low.

When the chicken is thoroughly cooked, use two forks to shred and serve with lime juice, cilantro and other optional toppings, if desired.

Butternut Squash and Chicken Stew

Prep time: 20 minutes | Cook time: 6-8 hours | Serves 4

Ingredients:

- 1 lb. chicken thighs, boneless, skinless, and cut into 1-inch pieces
- 8 oz. cremini
- mushrooms, sliced
- 2 carrots, diced
- 1 butternut squash, diced
- 1 onion, diced
- 2 tsp. gluten-free Worcestershire sauce
- 1 (14.5 oz.) can diced tomatoes
- 1 tsp. thyme
- 1 tsp. oregano
- Salt and freshly ground pepper, to taste.

Directions:

1. Add all ingredients to the slow cooker and cook on Low for 6 to 8 hours, or until the chicken is fully cooked.

Slow Cooker Drunken Chicken

Prep time: 20 minutes | Cook time: 4-6 hours | Serves 4

Ingredients:

- 2 lbs. boneless, skinless chicken breasts
- 1 cup raisins
- 3 cloves garlic, minced
- ¼ cup dry sherry
- ½ tsp. salt
- ½ tsp. freshly ground pepper
- 2 Tbsp. coconut oil
- 1 onion, diced
- 2 apples, diced
- 1 cup slivered almonds
- 1-2 plantains, (depending on the size) yellow with no black spots, sliced
- 2 cups chicken stock
- ½ cup tequila

Optional for serving: Additional vegetables of choice.

Directions:

1. Season the chicken with salt and pepper. Melt the coconut oil in a large skillet over medium-high heat and sear the chicken on both sides until golden brown.

2. Place in the slow cooker with the rest of the ingredients and cook on Low for 4-6 hours.

Slow Cooker Moroccan Chicken

Prep time: 20 minutes | Cook time: 4-6 hours | Serves 6

Ingredients:

- 3 lbs. chicken thighs, boneless and skinless
- 4 cloves garlic, minced
- 1 lbs. baby carrots
- 1 onion, chopped
- 1 tsp. ginger
- ¼ cup fresh cilantro
- 6 oz. dried apricots, chopped (no sugar added)
- 2 Tbsp. coconut oil
- ½ cup chicken stock
- ¼ cup creamy unsalted almond butter
- ¼ cup sliced almonds, roasted
- 1 tsp. salt
- 1 tsp. cumin
- ½ tsp. coriander
- ½ tsp. cinnamon
- ¼ tsp. cayenne
- ¼ tsp. freshly ground pepper

Directions:

1. Heat coconut oil in a large skillet over medium-high heat. Season the chicken well with salt and pepper, and then add half the chicken to the pan and seat. Brown on all sides about 5 minutes. Transfer the chicken to the slow cooker and repeat with remaining half chicken.

2. In the same pan, sauté the onion and garlic for 3 minutes or until tender. Add the ginger cumin, coriander, cinnamon, cayenne, salt, and pepper and cook for another minute.

3. Stir in the chicken stock and almond butter, and then pour over the chicken in the slow cooker. Cook on Low for 4 to 6 hours. Add the apricots and baby carrots to the slow cooker in the last hour of cooking.

Slow Cooker Chicken Cacciatore

Prep time: 20 minutes | Cook time: 4-6 hours | Serves 4-6

Ingredients:
- 3 lbs. chicken thighs, boneless and skinless
- 6 cloves garlic, minced
- 2 onions, minced
- 1 ½ lbs. cremini mushrooms, cut in half or quartered, if large
- ¼ cup fresh basil, chopped
- 2 Tbsp. butter or ghee
- 1 (14.2 oz.) can diced tomatoes, drained
- ½ oz. dried mixed wild mushrooms, minced
- ½ cup chicken stock
- ½ cup dry red wine
- 2 tsp. dried oregano
- ¼ cup tomato paste
- ¼ tsp. red pepper flakes
- Salt and freshly ground pepper, to taste

Directions:
1. Place all ingredients in the slow cooker, except for the basil. Cook on Low for 4 to 6 hours.
2. Serve with fresh basil on top.

Slow Cooker Tom Kha Gai

Prep time: 5-10 minutes | Cook time: 6 hours | Serves 4

Ingredients:
- 1 lbs. chicken breast, skinless and boneless and cut into thin slices
- 8 oz. mushrooms, sliced
- 3 Tbsp. fresh lime juice
- 2 Tbsp. fresh ginger, grated
- 1 lemongrass stalk, chopped into 1-inch pieces
- 4 cups chicken stock
- 3 Tbsp. coconut aminos
- 3 (14 oz.) cans full-fat coconut milk
- 2 tsp. yellow or green curry paste
- 1 to 2 tsp. fish sauce
- 1 Tbsp. honey
- Salt, to taste

Optional for serving: Cilantro, green onion, lime juice.

Directions:
1. Place all ingredients, except the cilantro and mushrooms, into the slow cooker and cook on Low for 6 hours.
2. Add the mushrooms during the last 30 minutes of cooking, and then top with cilantro green onion, and lime when serving.

Slow Cooker Cashew Chicken Curry

Prep time: 20 minutes | Cook time: 5-6 hours | Serves 4

Ingredients:

For the sauce:
- 1 tsp. fresh ginger, grated
- ½ onion, mined
- 2 Tbsp. cashew butter
- 2 Tbsp. coconut aminos
- 2 tsp. red Thai curry paste
- 1 (14 oz.) can full-fat coconut milk
- 1 tsp. honey
- 1 tsp. fish sauce
- 1 tsp. curry powder
- ¼ tsp. red pepper flakes

For the curry:
- 1 ½ lbs. chicken breasts or thighs, boneless and skinless
- 2 carrots, thinly sliced
- 1 cup cabbage, thinly sliced
- 1 lime, juiced
- 1 Tbsp. fresh Thai basil
- ½ red bell pepper, thinly sliced
- ¼ cup cilantro, chopped

Optional: for serving: Vegetables, lime juice, Basmati rice or cauliflower rice.

Directions:

1. Combine all sauce ingredients and mix well. Place the chicken in the slow cooker, then pour the sauce over it. Add the remaining ingredients except for the cabbage. Cook on Low for about 5 ½ to 6 hours and add the cabbage during the last 30 minutes.

Slow Cooker Enchilada Soup

Prep time: 5-10minutes | Cook time: 6-8 hours | Serves 4-6

Ingredients:

- 1 ½ lbs. boneless, skinless chicken breasts, cubed
- 3 cloves garlic, minced
- 1 onion, diced
- 1 bell pepper, diced
- 10 oz. gluten-free enchilada sauce
- 2 to 3 cups chicken stock
- 2 (14 oz.) can fire-roasted tomatoes
- 2 (4 oz.) cans diced green chiles
- 1 (14 oz.) can black beans, drained
- 1 small can sliced black olives
- 1 tsp. cumin
- 1 tsp. chili powder
- Salt, to taste

Optional for serving: Cilantro, avocado, red onion, shredded cheese, sour cream.

Directions:

1. Add all the ingredients to the slow cooker and stir. Cook on Low for 6 to 8 hours, or until the chicken is tender. Serve with any desired toppings.

Slow Cooker Sweet Potato and Chicken Korma

Prep time: 20 minutes | Cook time: 4 hours | Serves 4-6

Ingredients:

- 2 lbs. free-range chicken thighs, boneless and skinless
- 3 cloves garlic, minced
- 2 sweet potatoes, cubed
- 2 onions, sliced
- 2 Tbsp. coconut oil
- 2 tsp. honey
- 1 can full- fat coconut milk
- 1 Tbsp. coriander
- 1 Tbsp. cumin
- 1 tsp. salt
- 1 tsp. chili powder
- 1 tsp. paprika
- ½ tsp. turmeric
- 2 tsp. garam masala

Directions:

1. Combine the coriander, cumin, turmeric, chili powder, paprika garam masala, and salt in a small bowl. Add enough water to form a paste, about 1 Tbsp.

2. Melt the coconut oil in a large skillet over medium-low heat. Add the onions, garlic, and honey and sauté for 10 to 15 minutes. Add the spice paste and cook for another 2 minutes. Add the coconut milk and puree in a blender.

3. Pour the sauce into the slow cooker and add the chicken and sweet potato. Make sure the meat is coated and cook on Low for about 4 hours. Serve with rice or cauliflower rice, if desired.

Slow Cooker 40 Clove Chicken

Prep time: 10 minutes | Cook time: 8 hours | Serves 4-6

Ingredients:

- 5-7 lb. whole chicken
- 40 cloves garlic, whole and peeled
- 3 sprigs fresh rosemary
- 2 tsp. fresh thyme, minced
- 2 tsp. fresh sage, minced
- 2 Tbsp. coconut oil, melted
- ½ tsp. freshly ground pepper
- ½ tsp. salt

Optional for serving: Roasted vegetables and mashed potatoes.

Directions:

1. Rinse the chicken off and dry with a paper towel (make sure the giblets are removed from the body cavity). Place half of the garlic cloves inside the cavity and place breast side up in the slow cooker.
2. Rub the coconut oil all over the chicken. Sprinkle with the thyme, sage, salt, and pepper and massage it into the skin. Sprinkle the remaining garlic cloves around the chicken and add the sprigs or rosemary. Cook on Low for 8 hours.

Gently lift the chicken out of the slow cooker and let it rest for at least 15 minutes before carving. Serve with roasted vegetables and mashed potatoes with the cooking liquid poured over the top, if desired.

Slow Cooker Artichoke Chicken

Prep time: 15 minutes | Cook time: about 5 hours | Serves 4

Ingredients:

- 1 organic chicken, cut into pieces
- 1 container cremini mushrooms, quartered
- 2 cloves garlic, minced
- ½ onion, minced
- 1 (10 oz.) jar marinated artichoke hearts
- 8 oz. green olives, pitted
- ½ cup chicken stock
- Salt and freshly ground pepper, to taste

Optional for serving: Side salad or roasted vegetables.

Directions:

1. Pat the chicken pieces dry and sprinkle with Italian seasoning, salt, and pepper. Place in the slow cooker. Then add the remaining ingredients.

2. Cook on Low for 5 hours. After 5 hours, remove the chicken and vegetables from the slow cooker and place them in a large baking dish. Turn your broiler on High and broil for 10 minutes until the chicken skin is golden brown and crisp.

3. Serve with vegetables and any other desired sides.

Slow Cooker Honey Cashew Chicken

Prep time: 20 minutes | Cook time: about 3-4 hours | Serves 4-6

Ingredients:

- 1 ½ to 2 lbs. chicken breasts, boneless, skinless, and cut into pieces
- 2 cloves garlic, minced
- ½ onion, minced
- 3 Tbsp. coconut aminos
- 2 Tbsp. honey
- 2 Tbsp. tomato paste
- 2 Tbsp. water
- 2 tsp. arrowroot starch
- 1 ½ Tbsp. rice vinegar
- 1 cup cashews, ½ cup toasted and reserved for garnish
- 1 tsp. coconut oil
- 1 tsp. Siracha

Optional for serving: Sesame seeds, green onion, lime juice.

Directions:

1. Add honey, sesame oil, rice vinegar, coconut aminos tomato paste, onion garlic, and Siracha in a small bowl. Mix the water and arrowroot starch together, and then add it to the sauce.

2. Place the chicken and ½ cup of cashews in the slow cooker and pour the sauce on top. Cook on High 3 to 3 ½ hours.

3. Serve with vegetables and top with reserved toasted cashews, sesame seeds, scallions, and lime wedges, if desired.

Slow Cooker Tikka Masala

Prep time: 15 minutes | Cook time: 8 hours | Serves 4

Ingredients:

- 1 ½ lbs. chicken breast, boneless, skinless, and cut into pieces
- 4 cloves garlic, minced
- 1 onion, chopped
- 1 Tbsp. fresh ginger, grated
- 4 oz. full-fat plain Greek yogurt (no sugar added)
- 1 cup crushed tomatoes
- 1 cup full-fat coconut milk
- 1 Tbsp. cumin
- 1 Tbsp. garam masala
- 1 tsp. turmeric
- 1 tsp. coriander
- ½ tsp. cardamom
- ½ Tbsp. chili powder
- Salt, to taste

Optional for serving: Basmati or cauliflower rice, cilantro.

Directions:

1. Combine the chicken, ginger, onion, garlic, tomatoes, coconut milk, and spices in the slow cooker and cook on Low for 8 hours.

2. Stir a few spoonfuls of the tikka masala sauce (from the slow cooker) into the yogurt to bring the temperature up and prevent curdling. Once mixed, pour the yogurt mixture back into the slow cooker and stir. Let it thicken for 15 minutes. Taste and add salt as needed.

3. Serve over Basmati or cauliflower rice with cilantro on top.

Slow Cooker Honey Mustard Chicken

Prep time: 15 minutes | Cook time: 4-6 hours | Serves 4

Ingredients:

- 8 chicken thighs, bone-in and skin-on
- 2 heads broccoli, cut into florets
- 2 cloves garlic, minced
- Zest from 1 orange
- 2 Tbsp. unsalted butter
- 3 Tbsp. Dijon mustard
- 1 Tbsp. whole grain mustard
- 1 Tbsp. white wine vinegar
- ½ cup honey
- ½ tsp. rosemary
- ½ tsp. oregano
- Salt and freshly ground pepper, to taste.

Directions:

1. In a large bowl, whisk together the honey, mustards, white wine vinegar, garlic, rosemary, oregano, orange zest, salt, and pepper, then set aside.

2. Melt butter in a large skillet over medium-high heat. Add chicken, skin-side down and sear on both sides until golden brown - about 2 to 3 minutes per side.

3. Place the chicken thighs in the slow cooker. Stir in the sauce and cook on Low for 4 to 6 hours. Add broccoli during the last 30 minutes of cooking time.

Slow Cooker Orange Chicken

Prep time: 10 minutes | Cook time: about 5 hours | Serves 4

Ingredients:

- 2 lbs. chicken breast, boneless and skinless, cubed
- 2 oranges, freshly squeezed and zested
- 2 cloves garlic, minced
- 1 cup chicken stock
- ½ cup rice vinegar
- ½ cup coconut aminos
- ¼ cup honey
- ¼ cup tapioca starch
- 1 tsp. red pepper flakes
- ¼ tsp. ginger
- ¼ tsp. freshly ground black pepper

Optional for serving: Additional vegetables, white rice or cauliflower rice.

Directions:

1. Whisk together the sauce ingredients: stock, orange juice, honey, vinegar, coconut aminos, garlic, orange zest, red pepper flakes, ground ginger and black pepper.

2. Place the chicken in the slow cooker, pour the sauce over and toss the pieces to coat. Cook on Low for 4 hours.

3. Strain the liquid into a small sauce pan and whisk in the tapioca starch until no lumps remain. Place the pot over Medium heat and stir consistently until it thickens slightly. Add the chicken to the sauce and serve with cauliflower or white rice and any other desired vegetables.

Slow Cooker BBQ Chicken

Prep time: 10 minutes | Cook time: about 6 hours | Serves 4

Ingredients:
- 1 large chicken
- 3 cloves garlic, minced
- ½ onion, minced
- 3 Tbsp. honey
- 2 Tbsp. tomato paste
- 2 Tbsp. coconut oil
- 1 ½ cups apple cider vinegar
- ½ cup tomato sauce or crushed tomatoes
- 1 tsp. salt
- 1 tsp. freshly ground pepper
- 1 tsp. hot sauce of choice

Directions:
1. Place the chicken in the slow cooker and sprinkle with salt and pepper. Cook on High for 3 hours or on Low for about 5 hours. (You could also cook 1 ½ to 2 pounds of chicken breasts instead of a whole chicken, if you prefer.)
2. In a large saucepan, melt the coconut oil over medium heat. Add the minced onion and garlic and cook until softened, about 4 to 6 minutes.
3. Add the rest of the ingredients: apple cider vinegar, tomato sauce, tomato paste, honey, salt, black pepper, and hot sauce. Mix well and bring to a boil, and then lower heat to a simmer.
4. Simmer in the sauce until the volume has reduced between a quarter to a third. It should be slightly thick.
5. When the chicken is done cooking and has cooled a little, shred the meat and mix with the sauce.

Slow Cooker Pesto Chicken

Prep time: 10 minutes | Cook time: 4-6 hours | Serves 4

Ingredients:

- 1 ½ lbs. chicken breasts, boneless and skinless
- 2 cloves garlic, minced
- ½ onion, chopped
- 1 cup chicken stock
- Salt and freshly ground pepper, to taste

Pesto:
- 1 ½ cup spinach
- 1 cup fresh basil
- 1 clove garlic
- ½ lemon, juiced
- 3 Tbsp. olive oil
- ½ cup walnuts, or nut of choice.

Optional for serving: Parmesan cheese.

Directions:

1. Place the chicken in the slow cooker with the garlic, onion, stock, salt, and pepper. Cook on Low for 4 to 6 hours, or until it's fork tender.
2. Place all the pesto ingredients in the food processor and mix until smooth.
3. Once the chicken is removed and shredded or cubed, combine chicken and pesto in a bowl and serve.

Slow Cooker Chicken and Vegetable Soup

Prep time: 20 minutes | Cook time: 6-8 hours | Serves 4-6

Ingredients:

- 1 lb. Italian chicken sausage, diced
- 3 cloves garlic, minced
- 2 zucchinis, diced
- 2 celery stalks, diced
- 2 carrots, diced
- 1 lb. sweet potatoes, diced
- 1 onion, diced
- 1 tsp. fresh oregano, minced
- ½ lb. green beans, chopped
- 4 cups chicken stock
- 2 (14.5 oz.) cans fire-roasted tomatoes
- 2 bay leaves
- 1 pinch red pepper flakes
- Salt and freshly ground pepper, to taste

Directions:

1. Place all the ingredients in the slow cooker and cook on Low for 6 to 8 hours.

Slow Cooker Tuscan Chicken Soup

Prep time: 10 minutes | Cook time: 6-8 hours | Serves 6

Ingredients:

- 1 ½ lbs. cooked rotisserie chicken, shredded
- 4 cups baby spinach
- 4 cloves garlic, minced
- 3 carrots, diced
- 2 stalks celery, diced
- 1 onion, diced
- 6 cups chicken stock
- 2 (15 oz.) can Great Northern beans, drained and rinsed
- Salt and freshly ground pepper, to taste

Directions:

1. Place all ingredients in the slow cooker and cook on Low for 6 to 8 hours.

Slow Cooker Chicken Mole

Prep time: 20 minutes | Cook time: 6-8 hours | Serves 4

Ingredients:
- 2 lbs. chicken breasts or thighs, boneless and skinless
- 4 cloves garlic, chopped
- 1 onion, chopped
- 4 dried chilies (chilies de arbol)
- 2 cups organic canned tomatoes
- 2 Tbsp. unsweetened cocoa powder
- ½ cup raisins, no sugar added
- ¼ cup almonds
- 1 tsp. coriander
- ½ tsp. chili powder
- ½ tsp. cinnamon
- ½ tsp. guajillo chili powder
- 1 tsp. salt

Optional for serving: Avocado, cilantro, cabbage, jalapeño, shredded cheese, sour cream.

Directions:
1. In a large sauté pan, cook the onion, garlic, and spices until almost translucent, and then add the tomatoes, almonds and raisins and simmer with a lid for about 10 minutes.
2. Puree, and then put in the slow cooker with chicken and cook on Low for 6 to 8 hours. Serve with any desired toppings.

LAMB

Slow Cooker Braised Lamb Shanks

Prep time: 15 minutes | Cook time: 6-8 hours | Serves 4

Ingredients:

- 4 lamb shanks
- 4 cloves garlic, minced
- 2 celery stalks, died
- 2 carrots, diced
- 1 onion, diced
- 2 cups beef stock
- 2 Tbsp. tomato paste
- 1 (14 oz.) can of diced tomatoes
- 2 Tbsp. coconut oil
- 1 cup red wine
- 2 bay leaves
- 1 tsp. thyme
- Salt and freshly ground pepper, to taste

Optional for serving: Roasted parsnips, mashed potatoes, assorted vegetables.

Directions:

1. Place the onion, celery, carrots, garlic, stock, tomatoes, tomato paste, thyme, and bay leaf in the slow cooker.

2. Season the lamb with salt and pepper. Melt the coconut oil in a large skillet over medium-high heat and sear the meat on all sides. Add to the slow cooker. Place the pan back on the heat and add the wine. Simmer to 1 to 2 minutes before adding to the slow cooker.

Cook on Low for 6 to 8 hours. Serve with roasted vegetables and mashed potatoes, or any sides of your choice.

Slow Cooker Asian Inspired Lamb Stew

Prep time: 20 minutes | Cook time: 6-8 hours | Serves 4

Ingredients:

- 2 to 3 lbs. lamb shoulder, boneless and cut into 2-inch pieces
- 5 shallots, peeled and minced
- 4 garlic cloves, minced
- 4 carrots, roughly chopped
- 4 large tomatoes, roughly chopped
- 2 Thai chilies, seeds removed and finely chopped (optional)
- 1 butternut squash, peeled and cubed
- 1 lemongrass stalk, minced
- 1 Tbsp. fresh ginger, minced
- 2 ½ cups beef stock
- 2 Tbsp. coconut aminos
- 2 Tbsp. tomato paste
- 2 star anise
- 2 Tbsp. coconut oil
- 1 cinnamon stick
- 1 tsp. Chinese five-spice powder
- Salt and freshly ground pepper, to taste.

Directions:

1. In a large bowl, combine the lamb, coconut aminos, lemongrass, ginger, garlic, and salt and pepper to taste. Stir until everything is well coated. Refrigerate and marinate up to 8 hours.

2. In the slow cooker, place the carrots, butternut squash, cinnamon, star anise, Chinese five-spice, and beef stock. Melt coconut oil in large skillet placed over a medium-high heat and brown the lamb cubes on all sides. (You'll have to do this in a few batches to avoid overcrowding the pan.) Put the cooked meat on top of the veggies in the slow cooker.

3. In the same pan, lower the heat to medium, add the shallots and chilies, and cook another 2 to 3 minutes. Add the tomatoes and tomato paste, mix well, then add to the slow cooker. Set on Low and cook for 6 to 8 hours, or until the meat is tender.

PORK

Slow Cooker Hawaiian Pulled Pork

Prep time: 10 minutes | Cook time: 6-8 hours | Serves 8

Ingredients:

- 5 lbs. pork shoulder, boneless
- 1 head green cabbage, roughly chopped
- 1 ½ Tbsp. Red Hawaiian Sea Salt, or regular sea salt (for regular sea salt, use ½ to ¾ tsp. medium-coarse salt per pound of meat and ¼ to ½ tsp. fine salt per pound.)

Directions:

1. Rub the salt evenly over the pork and place in the slow cooker.
2. Set on Low and cook for 6 to 8 hours or until the meat is tender. Take the meat out of the liquid and shred, and remove any large pieces of fat.
3. Save a few tablespoons of the juice in the slow cooker and use it to cook the cabbage.

Slow Cooker Pork Roast with Apples

Prep time: 20 minutes | Cook time: 6-8 hours | Serves 4

Ingredients:

- 2 lbs. pork loin roast, boneless
- 4 cloves garlic, minced
- 3 apples, sliced
- 1 onion, roughly chopped
- 2 Tbsp. coconut oil
- 1 cup chicken stock
- ¼ cup honey
- 1 cinnamon stick
- Salt and freshly ground pepper, to taste

Directions:

1. Sprinkle salt and pepper on the pork.
2. Melt 2 tablespoons of coconut oil in a large skillet over high heat and seat the roast on all sides.
3. Cut 3-inch deep slits into the pork and insert an apple slice into each opening. Place the remaining apples, onions, and garlic in the bottom of the slow cooker and put the roast on top of the apples.
4. Drizzle the honey on top of the roast, and then add the chicken stock and cinnamon. Cook on Low for 6 to 8 hours or until the roast is for tender.

Slow Cooker Cassoulet

Prep time: 20 minutes | Cook time: 6-8 hours | Serves 6

Ingredients:
- 4 oz. bacon, cubed
- 3 links Spanish chorizo, sliced into ¼-inch coins
- 2 lbs. pork shoulder, cut into 1 ½-inch pieces
- 6 cloves garlic minced
- 1 onion, diced
- 1 Tbsp. fresh thyme
- 1 ½ Tbsp. salted butter
- 3 (15 oz.) cans Great Northern beans
- 2 Tbsp. tomato paste
- 1 ½ cups diced tomatoes
- 1 cup dry white wine
- 1 cup chicken stock
- Salt and freshly ground pepper, to taste

Directions:
1. Cook the bacon in a large skillet over medium heat until crisp, and then set aside. Season the pork with salt and pepper. Then brown all sides in the bacon fat and place in the slow cooker. (You'll probably have to do this in a few batches.)
2. Add the wine to the pan and simmer until it's reduced by half. Add in the tomato paste, chicken stock, and tomatoes. Simmer for 2 to 3 minutes, and then pour into the slow cooker along with the other remaining ingredients.
3. Cook on Low for 6 to 8 hours or until the pork is fork tender. Serve with a side salad or vegetable of your choice.

Slow Cooker Baby Back Ribs

Prep time: 20 minutes | Cook time: 7-8 hours | Serves 4

Ingredients:

- 4 lbs. pork baby back ribs
- 3 cloves garlic, minced
- 1 onion, minced
- 2 ½ cups ketchup
- 2 Tbsp. apple cider vinegar
- 2 tsp. coconut aminos
- ¼ cup honey
- 2 tsp. oregano.
- 1 Tbsp. chili powder
- 1 Tbsp. smoked paprika
- Salt and freshly ground pepper, to taste

Directions:

1. Preheat the oven to 400°F. Remove the membrane from the ribs by loosening it with a knife and peeling it off.
2. Season both sides of the ribs with salt and pepper and brown them in the oven for 10 to 12 minutes on each side. Then place them in the slow cooker
3. In a bowl, combine the ketchup, onion, chili powder, paprika, oregano, apple cider vinegar, coconut aminos, and honey. Season to taste with salt and pepper. Pour over the ribs and make sure they are coated well. Cook on Low for 7 to 8 hours.

Slow Cooker Pineapple Ham

Prep time: 10 minutes | Cook time: 6-8 hours | Serves 6-8

Ingredients:

- 6 to 8 lbs. bone-in ham, fully cooked
- 1 ½ cup fresh pineapple, cut into 1-inch pieces
- 2 Tbsp. Dijon mustard
- 1 (20 oz.) can pineapple rings
- ½ cup pineapple juice, no sugar added
- ½ cup honey
- ¼ cup chicken stock
- ¼ tsp. ground cloves
- ¼ tsp. nutmeg
- Salt and freshly ground pepper, to taste

Directions:

1. Place the ham in a slow cooker. Combine the pineapple juice, pineapple pieces, honey, mustard, cloves, and stock in a saucepan. Heat and stir until the honey is dissolved.

2. Pour the liquid over the ham and cook on Low for 6 to 8 hours. Baste with the cooking liquid every hour if possible.

3. Once the cooking time is up, preheat the broiler and place the ham in a baking dish. Arrange the pineapple slices on top of the ham, secure them with toothpicks, and brush the remaining sauce over the entire ham. Broil for 5 to 10 minutes right before serving.

Sausage, Pepper, and Cannellini Bean Stew

Prep time: 20 minutes | Cook time: about 8 hours | Serves 6-8

Ingredients:
- 5 links hot Italian sausage
- 3 cloves garlic
- 2 onions, chopped
- 2 red bell peppers, diced
- 2 carrots, diced
- 1 Tbsp. fresh basil
- 4 cups chicken stock
- 3 Tbsp. coconut oil
- 2 (15.5 oz.) cannellini beans, drained and rinsed
- 2 (14.5 oz.) fire-roasted tomatoes
- 1 tsp. oregano
- 1 tsp. fennel
- Salt and freshly ground pepper, to taste

Optional for serving: Freshly grated parmesan cheese.

Directions:
1. Melt coconut oil in a large skillet, and then sauté the onions, garlic, and peppers until they begin to soften. Then add to the slow cooker.
2. Take the sausages out of their casings and add to pan and brown well. Break into pieces and add to the slow cooker. Along with the remaining ingredients.
3. Cook on Low for 8 hours and serve with freshly grated parmesan cheese.

Slow Cooker Kale and Ham Hocks

Prep time: 15 minutes | Cook time: 6-8 hours | Serves 6-8

Ingredients:
- 1 smoked ham hock
- 12 cups kale, torn into 2-inch pieces
- 2 cloves garlic, minced
- 1 onion, thinly sliced
- 2 Tbsp. uncured bacon fat or coconut oil
- 2 Tbsp. apple cider vinegar
- 1 ½ cups water
- 1 cup chicken stock
- 1 pinch cayenne pepper
- Salt and freshly ground pepper, to taste

Directions:
1. Heat a large skillet over medium-high heat and add the bacon fat or coconut oil. Add the onion and sauté until it's translucent and lightly browned, about 5 to 8 minutes. Add the onions to the slow cooker, as well as the rest of the ingredients.
2. Cover and cook on Low for 6 to 8 hours.
3. Take the ham hock from the slow cooker and shred the meat, discarding the skin and bones. Add the meat back to the slow cooker and season with salt and pepper to taste.

Slow Cooker Carnitas

Prep time: 10 minutes | Cook time: 8-10 hours | Serves 8

Ingredients:

- 4 to 5 lbs. pork shoulder, boneless
- 5 to 7 cloves garlic, minced
- 2 limes, juiced
- 1 orange, juiced
- 2 Tbsp. salt
- 2 tsp. black pepper
- 1 tsp. cumin
- 2 tsp. chili powder
- 2 tsp. oregano
- ½ tsp. cayenne

Optional for serving: Lime juice, cilantro, shredded cabbage, avocado, beans, sour cream, shredded cheese.

Directions:

1. Trim off any excess fat from the pork. (It's OK to leave a little. It adds good flavor.) Mix all the dry spices together and rub it on all sides of the meat.
2. Place the meat into the slow cooker and add the garlic, lime, and orange juice.
3. Set on Low and cook for 8 to 10 hours. Once it's done cooking, shred the meat and discard any large pieces of fat. Serve with any additional toppings.

Slow Cooker Chile Verde

Prep time: 5-10minutes | Cook time: 6-8 hours | Serves 4-6

Ingredients:
- 2 lbs. pork roast, boneless and cubed
- 3 cloves garlic, minced
- 2 Anaheim chilies, seeds and ribs removed and chopped
- 1 to 2 jalapeños, diced
- 1 poblano pepper, seeds and ribs removed and chopped
- 1 onion, chopped
- 3 (4 oz.) cans diced green chilies
- 2 cup chicken stock
- 1 (8 oz.) can diced tomatoes
- 2 tsp. fresh oregano
- 1 tsp. salt
- 1 tsp. freshly ground pepper
- ½ tsp. cumin
- ½ tsp. paprika

Optional for serving: Limes, cilantro, shredded cabbage, avocado, beans, sour cream, shredded cheese.

Directions:
1. Combine all ingredients in the slow cooker and cook on Low for 6 to 8 hours. Shred meat and serve with any optional toppings, if desired.

SEAFOOD

Slow Cooker Crab Bisque

Prep time: 10 minutes | Cook time: 6-8 hours | Serves 4-6

Ingredients:

- 1 lb. fresh or frozen lump crabmeat (look over for shell pieces)
- 3 shallots, minced
- 3 cloves garlic, minced
- 2 stalks celery, minced
- 1 carrot, peeled and diced
- 1 sweet potato, cubed
- 1 lemon, juiced
- 2 cups heavy cream
- 1 Tbsp. salted butter
- 5 cups fish or chicken stock
- 1 tsp. paprika
- ½ tsp. cayenne
- Salt and freshly ground pepper, to taste

Directions:

1. Put all ingredients, except for the crab, in the slow cooker. Cook on Low for 6 to 8 hours, and then use an immersion blender to puree to the desired consistency. (Be careful transferring the hot liquid if you use a regular blender instead.)
2. Return the soup to the slow cooker and add the crab. Allow it to warm all the way through before serving.

Slow Cooker Pesto Halibut

Prep time: 10 minutes | Cook time: 2-4 hours | Serves 4

Ingredients:

- 2 lbs. white fish (cod, halibut, and so on)
- 6 to 8 oz. pesto
- ¼ to ½ cup shredded Parmesan cheese
- Salt and freshly ground pepper

Optional for serving: Assorted vegetables.

Directions:

1. Lay out 4 pieces of foil and place a fillet in the center of each. Spoon the pesto over the top and sprinkle with freshly ground pepper and parmesan cheese.
2. Fold the foil to seal the fish and place in the slow cooker and cook on Low for 2 to 4 hours. The fish is done when it flakes easily with a fork.
3. Serve with any vegetables or sides of your choice.

Slow Cooker Lemon Dill Salmon

Prep time: 10 minutes | Cook time: about 2 hours | Serves 4

Ingredients:

- 2 lbs. salmon, cut into 4 fillets
- 16 oz. fresh spinach
- 4 cloves garlic, minced
- 4 tsp. fresh dill
- 3 lemons, sliced
  into rounds
  (save one whole lemon serving)
- ¼ cup chicken or vegetable stock
- 2 Tbsp. olive oil
- Salt and freshly
  ground pepper, to taste

Directions:

1. Lay the spinach down in the bottom of the slow cooker, and then top with the salmon. Sprinkle the olive oil, herbs and minced garlic on top of each fillet.

2. Slice the lemons and place them on top of the fish, and then add the stock. Cook on Low for 2 hours, or until the fish flakes easily with a fork. Cook for less time depending on the desired doneness. Serve with the spinach, fresh lemon, and any other sides of your choice.

Slow Cooker Seafood Chowder

Prep time: 20 minutes | Cook time: about 6 hours | Serves 4

Ingredients:

- 6 slices bacon, diced
- 1 lb. firm white fish, cut into small cubes (cod, halibut, and so on)
- 1 lb. raw shrimp, shells and tails removed
- 2 cloves garlic, minced
- 1 lb. red potatoes, diced
- 1 onion, diced
- 1 cup celery, diced
- 1 jalapeño, seeded and diced
- 1 cup heavy cream
- 1 cup dry white wine
- 1 large can of clams, including the juice
- 1 tsp. thyme, minced
- 1 tsp. Cajun seasoning
- Salt and freshly ground pepper, to taste

Optional for serving: ½ cup chopped fresh parsley.

Directions:

1. Cook the bacon until crispy. Remove the pan and sauté the onion, celery, and garlic until translucent. Add the spices and wine and boil for 2 to 3 minutes.

2. Pour mixture into the slow cooker. Add the potatoes and cook on Low for 6 hours. Add the clams and juice, fish, shrimp, bacon, jalapeño, and cream. Cook on High for another 10 to 20 minutes until all the seafood is cooked through. Serve with parsley on top, if desired.

Slow Cooker Jambalaya

Prep time: 15 minutes | Cook time: about 6 hours | Serves 4

Ingredients:
- 6 oz. chicken, diced
- 1 lb. raw large shrimp, peeled and deveined
- 1 package Andouille sausage, sliced
- 4 bell peppers, diced (any color)
- 4 cloves garlic, diced
- 2 cups frozen okra (optional)
- 1 head cauliflower, food-processed into rice-sized pieces (you can substitute regular rice for the cauliflower)
- 1 onion, diced
- 5 cups chicken stock
- 1 (14.5 oz.) can diced tomatoes
- 3 Tbsp. Cajun seasoning
- 2 bay leaves
- ¼ cup hot sauce

Directions:
1. Place all ingredients in the slow cooker except for the sausage, shrimp, and cauliflower (or regular rice). Cook on Low for about 6 hours. With 30 minutes of cooking time left, add the sausage, shrimp, and cauliflower rice. If using regular rice, cook separately as the package directs.

Serve over additional cauliflower or regular rice, if desired.

VEGETABLES

Slow Cooker Red Lentil Curry

Prep time: 15 minutes | Cook time: 7-8 hours | Serves 6-8

Ingredients:
- 5 cloves garlic, minced
- 2 onions, diced
- 1 Tbsp. ginger, minced
- 4 Tbsp. salted butter
- 4 cups brown lentils
- 4 Tbsp. red curry paste
- 2 (29 oz.) cans tomato puree
- 1 qt. chicken stock
- ½ cup full-fat coconut milk
- 1 ½ tsp. turmeric
- 1 Tbsp. garam masala
- 1 tsp. salt
- ¼ tsp. cayenne pepper

Optional for serving: Fresh cilantro or parsley.

Directions:
1. Rinse the lentils well, and then put them in the slow cooker. Add the rest of the ingredients except for the coconut milk and cook on Low for 7 to 8 hours.
2. Stir in the coconut milk at the end and serve with cilantro or parsley on top.

Slow Cooker French Onion Soup

Prep time: 10 minutes | Cook time: 18-20 hours | Serves 4-6

Ingredients:

- 3 lbs. onion, thinly sliced
- 2 Tbsp. unsalted grass-fed butter, melted
- 10 cups beef stock (or chicken or vegetable)
- 2 Tbsp. balsamic vinegar
- 2 Tbsp. olive oil
- 1 tsp. salt, plus more to taste
- Freshly ground pepper
- 1 ½ to 2 cups Gruyere cheese, grated (optional)
- Fresh organic chives, chopped (optional)

Directions:

1. Put the onion slices in the slow cooker. Stir in the butter, olive oil, salt, and pepper. Cook on Low for 12 hours. The onions should be browned and soft.
2. Add the stock and balsamic vinegar. Cook on Low for 6 to 8 hours. Taste for seasoning.

Turn the broiler on and the ladle soup into individual bowls. Top each bowl with a baguette slice and cheese, if using. Broil for 2 to 3 minutes, or until the cheese is bubbling and browned

Slow Cooker Minestrone

Prep time: 20 minutes | Cook time: 6-8 hours | Serves 4

Ingredients:

- 3 cloves garlic, minced
- 2 celery stalks, diced
- 2 zucchinis, diced
- 2 carrots, diced
- 1 onion, diced
- 5 to 6 cups chicken stock
- 2 Tbsp. tomato paste
- 1 cup dry white wine
- 1 (28 oz.) can diced tomatoes
- 1 (14.5 oz.) can crushed tomatoes
- 1 (15 oz.) can kidney beans
- 1 cup gluten-free rice pasta
- ¼ cup pesto
- 2 bay leaves
- 2 tsp. Italian seasoning
- Salt and freshly ground pepper, to taste.

Optional for serving: ¼ cup grated parmesan cheese and fresh basil.

Directions:

1. Add all ingredients except the pasta to the slow cooker and cook on Low for 6 to 8 hours. Cook the pasta separately as the package directs. Add the pasta to the soup right before serving.
2. Serve with thinly sliced basil and parmesan cheese on top, if desired.

Slow Cooker Butternut Squash Soup

Prep time: 20 minutes | Cook time: 6-8 hours | Serves 4-6

Ingredients:
- 6 slices uncured bacon, cooked and crumbled
- 6 cups butternut squash, diced
- 2 large carrots, diced
- 2 apples, diced
- 1 leek, rinsed well and chopped
- 1 clove garlic, minced
- 1 tsp. fresh sage
- 1 tsp. fresh thyme
- 2 cups chicken stock (or more if needed)
- 1 cup full-fat coconut milk
- ½ tsp. salt
- ¼ tsp. black pepper.

Optional for serving: Fresh chives, chopped.

Directions:
1. Put the squash, apples, carrots, leek, garlic, stock and herbs in the slow cooker cook on Low for 6 to 8 hours.
2. Once the squash is fork tender, transfer to a blender and blend until smooth. (Be careful, it will be very hot!) You can also use an immersion blender to blend the soup. Add in coconut milk and additional stock if you want it to have a thinner consistency.
3. Add more salt and pepper to taste if necessary. Serve with chopped bacon and chives.

DESSERT

Slow Cooker Pumpkin Custards

Prep time: 10 minutes | Cook time: 4-6 hours | Serves 4-6

Ingredients:

- 6 eggs
- 3 cups canned pumpkin
- 2 Tbsp. coconut oil
- ¼ cup full-fat coconut milk
- ¼ cup maple syrup
- 2 tsp. vanilla extract
- 1 to 2 Tbsp.
  pumpkin pie spice
- ¼ tsp. salt

Optional for serving:
Heavy cream, whipped.

Directions:

1. Fill the slow cooker with 1 inch of water and turn on High
   and allow it to preheat for 45 to 60 minutes.

In a blender, puree all the ingredients. Pour into oven/heat-
proof ramekins or mason jars (fill about 2/3 full.) Carefully
place them in the water and cook on Low for 4 to 6 hours, or
until the filling is no longer jiggly. If there isn't enough room,
the jars can be stacked. Serve as is or with a dollop of freshly
whipped cream.

Slow Cooker Oatmeal Chocolate Chip Cookie Bars

Prep time: 10 minutes | Cook time: 2.5 hours | Serves 12

Ingredients:
- 4 to 5 Medjool dates, finely chopped
- 2 eggs
- 2 Tbsp. chia seeds
- 1 ½ cups gluten-free rolled oats
- ½ cup dark chocolate chips
- ½ cup maple syrup
- ½ cup coconut butter
- ¼ cup flax meal
- ¼ cup shredded unsweetened coconut
- ½ tsp. baking powder
- 2 tsp. vanilla extract
- ½ tsp. salt

Directions:
1. In bowl, combine all the dry ingredients and then combine all the wet in another. Add the wet to the dry and mix until everything is combined.
2. Lightly oil the inside of the slow cooker with coconut oil and line with parchment paper on the bottom and about one inch up the sides.
3. Evenly spread out the batter and cook on Low for about 2 ½ hours. Once the bars are done, remove them from the slow cooker and allow to cool before cutting.

Slow Cooker Chocolate Sundae Pudding

Prep time: 15 minutes | Cook time: about 2 hours | Serves 4-6

Ingredients:

Cake:

- ½ cup milk (almond or coconut milk will also work)
- 2 Tbsp. coconut oil, melted
- 2 Tbsp. unsweetened cocoa powder
- 1 cup gluten-free flour
- 1 ½ tsp. baking powder
- ½ cup dark chocolate chips
- ½ cup coconut sugar
- 2 tsp. vanilla extract

Toppings:

- 2 Tbsp. unsweetened cocoa powder
- 1 ½ cup boiling water
- ¾ cup coconut sugar

Optional for serving: Heavy cream, whipped.

Directions:

1. Lightly oil the inside of the slow cooker. In a bowl, combine the flour, coconut sugar, cocoa powder, and baking powder. Add the milk, oil or butter, and vanilla and lightly mix. Stir in the chocolate chips, and then spoon batter into the slow cooker.

2. In another bowl, mix the remaining ¾ cup coconut sugar and cocoa powder. Add the boiling water and stir. Pour this mixture over the batter in the slow cooker but do not stir!

3. Cook on High for 2 hours, or until a toothpick inserted into the center of the cake comes out clean. Turn the slow cooker off and take off the lid. Let cake sit for 30 minutes to cool.

4. Serve with ice cream or whipped cream, if desired.

Slow Cooker Apple Crisp

Prep time: 15 minutes | Cook time: about 4 hours | Serves 6

Ingredients:

Apples:

- 8 Braeburn or Granny Smith Apples, cored and sliced
- 1 lemon, juiced
- ¾ cup coconut sugar
- 2 tsp. cinnamon
- 1 tsp. vanilla extract

Topping:

- 8 Tbsp. unsalted cutter, melted
- ½ cup gluten-free rolled oats
- ½ cup gluten-free all purpose flour
- ½ cup coconut sugar
- 1 tsp. cinnamon
- 1 tsp. salt

Optional for serving: Heavy cream (whipped) or ice cream.

Directions:

1. Place the sliced apples in the slow cooker and toss with the lemon juice, cinnamon, coconut sugar, and vanilla

2. In a small bowl, combine the butter, oats, flour blend, coconut sugar, cinnamon, and salt. Stir to combine all ingredients. Crumble the dough on top of apples evenly.

3. Cook on Low for 3 hours, and then cook for another hour with the lid partially open. Serve with ice cream or freshly whipped cream.

Slow Cooker Cheesecake

Prep time: 15 minutes | Cook time: 2-3 hours | Serves 6-8

Ingredients:

Curst:

- ½ cup Medjool dates
- 2 Tbsp. Coconut oil, melted
- ½ cup almonds
- ½ cup pecans
- ½ cup unsweetened coconut flakes

Filling:

- 16 oz. cream cheese
- 2 eggs
- ¼ cup heavy cream
- 1 cup coconut sugar
- 1 tsp. vanilla extract

Directions:

1. Blend the dates in a food processor until they become smooth paste. Remove and add the nuts. Pulse until they are a coarse meal. Add to the dates and stir in the coconut oil. Mix until well incorporated, then press evenly into the bottom of an 8-inch spring form pan.

2. Combine the filling ingredients together until smooth and no lumps remain. Pour over the crust and place the dish inside the slow cooker insert. Pour about 1 ½ inches of water in the slow cooker to surround the baking dish. This will help the cheesecake cook evenly.

3. Cook on High for 2 to 3 hours. Check after 1 hour. You'll see the cheesecake is done when the edges are set and the center is no longer jiggly. Chill in the refrigerator before serving.

Slow Cooker Tapioca Pudding

Prep time: 10 minutes | Cook time: 5-6 hours | Serves 8

Ingredients:

- 3 eggs
- 2 qts. Milk (coconut milk will work too)
- 1 ½ cups coconut sugar
- 1 cup small pearl tapioca
- 1 tsp. vanilla extract

Directions:

1. Combine the milk, coconut sugar, and tapioca pearls in the slow cooker. Stir well and cook on High for 2 to 5 hours. The tapioca will be soft and kind of slimy.

2. In a bowl, whisk the eggs with the vanilla. Take ½ cup of the tapioca mixture and whisk it into the egg bowl. (This helps temper the eggs so they don't curdle.) Add another ½ cup and whisk well. Pour that mixture into the slow cooker and mix that until incorporated.

3. Cook on High for another 30 to 45 minutes, or until the tapioca is thick, pudding consistency. Unplug and allow it sit for about an hour to cool before placing in the refrigerator.

Slow Cooker Fudge

Prep time: 10 minutes | Cook time: about 2 hours | Serves 8

Ingredients:

- 2 ½ cups dark chocolate chips
- 1/3 cup full-fat coconut milk
- ¼ cup maple syrup
- 1 tsp. vanilla extract (or any other flavor would be good)

Directions:

1. Mix all ingredients in the slow cooker. Cover and cook on Low for 2 hours.
2. Uncover and cook 1 more hour. Stir well for about 5 minutes, and then pour into a parchment lined baking dish refrigerate for 1 to 2 hours. Slice and serve.